SCRIBE PUBLICATIONS

THE BEST OF BRITAIN'S POLITICAL CARTOONS 2014

Tim Benson is the world's leading authority on political cartoons. He runs The Political Cartoon Gallery, the world's largest website for the sale of original cartoon art, and regularly curates exhibitions at his Cartoon Café in Eastbourne, UK. He has produced numerous books on political cartoonists, including *Churchill in Caricature*, *Low and the Dictators*, *The Cartoon Century: modern Britain through the eyes of its cartoonists*, and *Drawing the Curtain: the Cold War in cartoons*. He is presently working on *Over The Top: a cartoon history of Australia at war* to commemorate the 100th anniversary of the Gallipoli landings in April 2015.

THE BEST OF BRITAIN'S POLITICAL CARTOONS 2014

EDITED BY TIM BENSON

SCRIBE

Melbourne • London

Scribe Publications
18–20 Edward St, Brunswick, Victoria 3056, Australia
2 John St, Clerkenwell, London, WC1N 2ES, United Kingdom

First published by Scribe 2014

Front-cover image: Morten Morland
Back-cover image: Steve Bright 'Brighty'

Printed and bound in the UK by CPI Group (UK) Ltd, Croydon CR0 4YY

National Library of Australia
Cataloguing-in-Publication data

Benson, Tim, editor.

The Best of Britain's Political Cartoons 2014.

9781922247643 (pbk.)

1. Political cartoons. 2. English wit and humor, Pictorial. 3. Great Britain–Politics and
government–Caricatures and cartoons.

320.9410207

scribepublications.com.au
scribepublications.co.uk

INTRODUCTION

DO POLITICIANS ACTUALLY ENJOY BEING DEPICTED IN political cartoons? Steve Bell, for one, thinks not. He told me that all the politicians he had discussed it with made out that they loved it, but he feels the reality is that they do not at all enjoy being visually ridiculed. However, Winston Churchill seemed to think politicians did indeed like it, and he would have known better than most. In a career spanning almost 60 years of front-line politics, he became the most cartooned political figure in the history of editorial cartooning. Churchill believed that being featured in a cartoon emphasised a politician's importance. On the contrary, politicians, according to Churchill, should be more concerned when they stopped appearing in them, as he noted:

'Just as eels are supposed to get used to skinning, so politicians get used to being caricatured. In fact, by a strange trait in human nature they even get to like it. If we must confess it, they are quite offended and downcast when the cartoons stop ... They murmur: "We are not mauled and maltreated as we used to be." The great days are ended.'

Former Labour MP and peer Manny Shinwell also believed this to be the case, as he once put it to former *Daily Express* cartoonist Michael Cummings: 'My boy, however angry politicians may get by the way you draw them in your cartoons, they'll be more angry if you leave them out!' The caricaturist Gerald Scarfe has stated that

A CARTOON FOR A DISSATISFIED CUSTOMER

David Low's 1950 cartoon makes light of readers' concerns that he does not treat political leaders with the respect they feel they deserved.

sometimes his 'victims' turned out to be fans, adding: 'They would rather be noticed than not noticed, even if it is a lousy depiction.' Disgraced former Labour MP Denis MacShane, when Europe minister in the Blair government, was absolutely thrilled at being depicted for the first time by Martin Rowson in *The Guardian*. He not only telephoned the cartoonist that morning to request the purchase of the original, but also begged Rowson to include him in more of his cartoons in the future.

Before the advent of television and when radio was

still in its infancy, cartoonists were, as a result, far more influential than today. Believe it or not, politicians would regularly encourage cartoonists to draw them by using what David Low termed 'tags of identity'. For example, former Conservative prime minister Stanley Baldwin was keen to be depicted smoking his pipe, which he believed gave him an affinity with the common man. Other politicians promoted their image for the benefit of the cartoonist, even if it was detrimental to their person. For example, former Conservative leader and foreign secretary Austen Chamberlain, in an attempt to emulate his famous father, Joseph, would wear only a monocle, even though he was dreadfully shortsighted. This meant that he could barely recognise people at a distance greater than a few feet. On one occasion, while sitting for David Low, Chamberlain asked, 'Must I wear my monocle? I cannot see to read with it very well.' Such blatant attempts by politicians to portray themselves in a favourable light explain why Churchill became so keen to promote himself this way using cigars, hats, and, of course, the 'V' sign.

Cartoonists occasionally even complained about prominent politicians who had no tags of identity. For example, Harold Wilson and David Low were members of the same golf club. At a chance meeting in the clubhouse, Low complained directly to Wilson, who, according to the former prime minister, 'shook his head sadly at him because he couldn't find anything in him to seize onto'. Within weeks, Wilson, like Baldwin before him, was suddenly seen everywhere with a pipe in his mouth.

Some cartoonists have been very successful over the years in getting under the skins of major political figures. It seems to help that those politicians who reach the top of the greasy pole appear to lose any self-deprecating sense of humour they may have had when

Unlike Michael Heseltine who loved being depicted in cartoons as Tarzan, John Major hated it, especially when drawn wearing underpants over his trousers.

they began their ascent. The pressure of being a front-line politician means they somehow become incapable of laughing at themselves. Former Labour prime minister James Callaghan was so disturbed by *The Sun*'s Stanley Franklin's continued depiction of him as the ever-hopeful Wilkins Micawber from Dickens' *David Copperfield* that he confronted the cartoonist directly. Franklin's defence was that it was the prerogative of the press to attack the prime minister. Callaghan's exasperated response was, 'Yes, I know, but every day?'

Sir Norman Fowler told me that John Major (once his junior minister) was very sensitive to being ridiculed in cartoons while prime minister. Major was particularly hurt by Steve Bell's portrayal of him as an ineffective Superman sporting Y-fronts over his trousers. 'These cartoons are done to destabilise me, so I ignore them,' he purportedly told a colleague. Major was also upset by *Spitting Image*'s depiction of him as a dull, boring, grey puppet whose only pleasure in life was enjoying a meal of peas with his wife, Norma. A frustrated Major told Matthew Parris that he 'hated peas!!!' This would not have displeased the creator of *Spitting Image*, Roger Law, who felt he had failed if any politicians actually liked the puppet of themselves. For example, former Conservative minister John Gummer paid a fortune for his *Spitting Image* puppet. On the other hand, former Conservative home secretary Kenneth Baker hated the puppet of himself as a greasy slug leaving a trail of slime wherever it went. Consequently, Baker said of *Spitting Image* that it, 'lacked subtlety and wit — it was an art form that destroyed itself by its own cruelty. It kicked people and figuratively cut off their arms and legs.' Of course, there was no love lost on either side. I once heard Roger Law say on radio that, given the chance, he would have 'loved to have taken a claw hammer to Baker'.

Another Conservative politician who despised the way he was depicted in cartoons was F.E. Smith, later Lord Birkenhead. While Conservative attorney-general in the 1920s, Smith complained bitterly to the proprietor of the *Evening Standard*, Lord Beaverbrook, about his paper's cartoonist, David Low:

'Your cartoonist over a long period of time published filthy and disgusting cartoons of me which were intended and calculated to do me great injury ... I know about modern caricature and I never had cause for grievance until you, a friend, allowed a filthy little socialist to present me daily as a crapulous and corpulent buffoon.'

Low was obviously highly effective at getting up the nose of senior Conservative politicians, as, at roughly at the same time, prime minister Stanley Baldwin referred

Dame Mary Soames views the original Illingworth Punch cartoon that so upset her father at the Political Cartoon Gallery in 2005.

to Low as 'evil and malicious'. Churchill also bitterly attacked Low as a scoundrel, who he said, never drew a single line in praise of England'. There were even times in 1940, when Churchill, under enormous pressure due to Britain's precarious position, believed Low was a dangerous subversive, doing great harm to the morale of the country.

In fact, Winston Churchill's vanity was notably pricked by another great cartoonist, Leslie Illingworth after a cartoon he drew for *Punch* in 1953 suggested it was time the then 78-year-old prime minister retired. The cartoon, titled 'Man goeth forth unto his work and to his labour until the evening', showed Churchill listless at his desk, with his face showing the unmistakable effects of a partial paralysis he had suffered the preceding summer. Churchill was bitterly hurt by the cartoon because it showed him as he truly was, not as he wanted to be portrayed. Churchill said of the cartoon: 'Yes, there's malice in it. Look at my hands — I have beautiful hands … Punch goes everywhere. I shall have to retire if this sort of thing goes on.' Churchill's doctor, Lord Moran, though, noticed the truth in the cartoon: 'The eyes were dull and lifeless. There was no tone in the flaccid muscles; the jowl sagged. It was the expressionless mask of extreme old age.' Malcolm Muggeridge, who, as editor of *Punch*, had given the go-ahead for the cartoon, became well known later in Churchill's circles as 'Buggeridge'.

However, no cartoonist was ever successful in antagonising Margaret Thatcher, the one prime minister who Steve Bell had referred to as the true 'antichrist'. I spoke to a number of Thatcher's former ministers to find out why. They all told me that, apart from obviously being very intelligent, she did not have a great sense of humour and, most importantly, did not understand irony. As a consequence, the visual barbs went straight over her head. Matthew Parris told me that, in any case, she refused to look at cartoons of herself. Her PR people, colleagues, and even her family were instructed not to show her any disrespectful or hurtful cartoons.

Politicians generally only acquire original cartoons of themselves that flatter them. During his long career in politics, Michael Heseltine built up a huge collection of original cartoons that depicted him as Tarzan. It must have obviously suited his purpose to be projected as lord of the 'political' jungle. Andrew Mitchell, MP, bought a number of original cartoons in 2013 in reference to the 'Plebgate' affair, of which he was at the centre. He told me, in reference to the affair, 'There have been horrible cartoons of me and some nice ones. I buy the nice ones.' It is no surprise that the disgraced Conservative peer Jeffrey Archer has built up a large collection of cartoons

— but, *guess what*, has none of himself.

When politicians do complain about the way they are drawn, it is usually more for reasons of vanity than of criticism of their policies. Politicians tend to be highly sensitive about how they look in cartoons. In the 1960s, Labour leader Hugh Gaitskell bemoaned the way he was caricatured by 'Vicky', even asking the cartoonist's colleague at the *Evening Standard*, Milton Shulman, to speak to Vicky about the way he drew Gaitskell's nose. 'He makes it look like a ski run,' Gaitskell told Shulman, running his fingers down his nose. 'It's not sharp at all. Can't he be more accurate?'

I held the opinion that Tony Blair was indifferent to ridicule by the cartoonists and thus just ignored it. However, according to Nick Brown, one of his former ministers, this was not the case. Blair was indeed incredibly vain about his appearance. As a defence mechanism, he would affect indifference. Brown added that Blair always wanted to appear 'masculine'. What Blair especially hated was being drawn with oversized ears and an ever-receding hairline. According to Brown, Steve Bell and Martin Rowson's cartoons in *The Guardian* especially got under Blair's skin.

The last two prime ministers, Gordon Brown and David Cameron, have both been particularly touchy in regard to cartoonists making them appear overweight. This really has struck a raw nerve with both men. Dave Brown, of *The Independent*, said that he had briefly met Gordon Brown when he was prime minister. He had said to him, 'You draw me far too fat. I'm not that fat.' Martin Rowson met Gordon Brown when he was chancellor, and recounted a similar conversation: 'He replied to my various points of policy by saying, "Why do you draw me so fat?" I think I said it was because he was fat. He made his excuses and left.'

Former *Daily Telegraph* cartoonist Nick Garland has said that Brown should have been flattered by the way he has been portrayed in cartoons. 'All of us drew Brown as hulking and big. He should take that as a compliment. He is a heavyweight figure, a presence.' Garland also said that it was preferable to the way William Hague has been depicted, 'as an ever-shrinking gnome' despite being 6 foot and 1 inch tall. Hague is another politician who has been riled by his depiction. He used to complain to the cartoonists that they drew him too small, pointing out to them that he was about the same height as Tony Blair. The reason for his 'smallness' had more to do with the then public's perception of him. According to cartoonist Dave Brown, it was 'because of his insignificance as Tory leader at a time when his party offered no genuine challenge to Labour'. As a consequence, every cartoonist would always draw him much smaller than Blair — and usually in the form of a child or schoolboy. As a result of his treatment, Hague has become contemptuous of cartoonists, having once told me, 'They, in any case, invariably get it wrong.'

Before he became prime minister, David Cameron seemed naively keen on being depicted in cartoons. In 2009, Cameron was 'intrigued' when I informed him that I was putting on an exhibition of original cartoons of him, titled *Cameron in Caricature,* at my Political Cartoon Gallery in London. He immediately sent one of his flunkeys down to see the exhibition, with the idea of using one of these cartoons as a Christmas card for himself. The flunkey was disappointed to find that the cartoons mercilessly ridiculed Cameron; the idea was, not surprisingly, quickly dropped.

As I mentioned in last year's cartoon anthology, *The Best of Britain's Political Cartoons 2013,* Cameron has been greatly irked by Steve Bell's depictions of him

David Cameron complained to *The Times* about the size of his bottom in this cartoon.'

with a condom over his head. Cameron foolishly told Bell, 'You can only push a condom so far.' This proved disastrously counter-productive. First, it showed that Bell had touched a raw nerve, and second, it only encouraged the cartoonist to continue using the condom motif.

Like Brown, Cameron has been equally sensitive about being depicted as fat. He complained to *The Times* when Peter Brookes drew him naked and with a bigger bottom than the rest of his cabinet. Christian Adams of the *The Daily Telegraph* recently met Cameron at a function, where the prime minister complained to him about the way he also drew him: 'Why do you draw me so fat? I'm not fat. Look at Michael Gove over there. He's much fatter than I am, but you don't draw him as fat; only me you depict as fat.' Adams responded by telling the prime minister he did not help himself by wearing such a tight-fitting running kit when out jogging!

THE CARTOONS

Gary Barker
The Guardian
24 August 2013

On 21 August, Bashar al-Assad's regime used the nerve gas sarin to kill hundreds of Syrian civilians, crossing the 'red line' that Barack Obama had said would prompt a United States military response.

Peter Brookes
The Times
31 August 2013

Labour voted against the House of Commons motion on whether Britain should intervene militarily in Syria. Downing Street accused the Labour leader Ed Miliband of 'buggering around' and 'playing politics' rather than responding 'seriously' to the crisis in Syria. Labour responded claiming that it was David Cameron's 'Flashman' approach and his 'character' failings, rather than Labour's actions, that explained his humiliation in his Commons defeat.

Chris Riddell
The Observer
1 September 2013

For many, the spectre of Tony Blair's 2003 decision to invade Iraq and oust Saddam Hussein had hung over the debate on whether to militarily intervene in Syria. In the fallout, David Cameron tried to position himself as a pragmatist, rather than an idealist. In his speech to the Commons, he had said that this situation was different from Iraq. 'I am deeply mindful of previous interventions,' he said. Thanks to Iraq and Afghanistan, the well of public confidence had been poisoned.

Dave Brown
The Independent
6 September 2013

United States president Barack Obama cancelled a meeting with Russian president Vladimir Putin in Moscow after Russia granted temporary asylum to NSA leaker Edward Snowden. The US decision was a diplomatic snub to Russia amid heightened tensions between the two countries over recent issues listed by the White House as 'missile defence and arms control, trade and commercial relations, global security issues, and human rights and civil society in the last 12 months.'

Peter Schrank
The Independent on Sunday
8 September 2013

The United States secretary of state John Kerry stated that not responding to the alleged use of chemical weapons by the Syrian regime was riskier than military strikes: 'I don't believe that we should shy from this moment: the risk of not acting is greater than the risk of acting.' Kerry said it was Assad who would not negotiate as long as he was not prevented from using chemical weapons: 'If one party believes he can rub out countless numbers of his own citizens with impunity he will never come to a negotiating table.' According to the cartoonist: Cartoons like this one don't have to be funny. They should, on the whole, provoke an emotional reaction.

Martin Rowson
The Guardian
9 September 2013

Ed Miliband told the TUC conference that he would press ahead with his decision to reform Labour's link with the trade unions. Many in the Labour Party feared such action would not help their poll ratings and would instead damage union support for the party, as well as cost Labour millions in much-needed battle funds in the run up to the next general election.

According to the cartoonist: The Cameron specs had just made their first tentative public appearance at the despatch box, all the better to read his briefing notes. Much talk was heard of whether they would add gravitas or interfere with his action-man demeanour. Either way, they were a blow to his vanity, just like with Blair before him. And vanity has been the driving factor of Cameron's tenure; remember that his reason for going for the top job was that he thought he'd 'be rather good at it', a statement almost Gladstonian in its demonstration of selfless civic duty. He was also known to 'chillax' with computer games on his iPad, notably 'Fruit Ninja' and 'Angry Birds', no doubt at the expense of his red boxes.

Andy Davey
The Sun
12 September 2013

14

THE QUEEN'S HEAD...

NOT EVEN MAGGIE COULD GET AWAY WITH THIS!

PRIVATISATION

SATIRICALSKETCHES.COM

Ben Jennings
i newspaper
14 September 2013

According to the cartoonist: This cartoon was in response to the privatisation of the Royal Mail by the Coalition. This is something that not even Maggie Thatcher could bring herself to do, saying she didn't want the 'Queen's head privatised'. I'd just got back from Amsterdam when I produced this piece and had seen some wonderful classic paintings whilst I was there at the Rijksmuseum, including a biblical one of Salome holding the head of John the Baptist on a platter, which inspired this cartoon.

Patrick Blower
The Daily Telegraph
14 September 2013

Newly released data from the Reuters/Ipsos MORI Political Monitor showed that the Liberal Democrats were seen as the most-divided party (65%) and least likely to keep their promises (16%). Only a quarter thought the Lib Dems were fit to govern.

Scott Clissold
Sunday Express
15 September 2013

The Conservatives pulled level with their Labour opposition for the first time in 18 months, according to a YouGov poll, as the economy started to show signs of recovery. Labour's lead had been steadily shrinking after rows about party funding, which had led to questions over Ed Miliband's leadership and a resulting slide in his personal ratings.

Steve Bell
The Guardian
19 September 2013

The Liberal Democrat president Tim Farron lavished praise on Ed Miliband: 'I really like Ed Miliband, so I don't want to diss him. I don't want to join in with the Tories who compare him to Kinnock.' A Liberal Democrat Voice poll showed, by 55% to 18%, that members would prefer a post-2015 alliance with Labour than one with the Tories.

Chris Riddell
The Guardian
22 September 2013

Asked about the claim by Ed Balls that the Labour party had become too macho under Gordon Brown and Tony Blair in the 1990s, Ed Miliband replied: 'I'm not sure I've ever been accused of being macho. I think that is a first. I think there are definitely lessons to be learned from the past.' At the Labour conference, Miliband dismissed poor opinion polls as he said he would focus on the increasing costs of living. 'Polls go up and down — one thing that goes up and up is the cost of living for ordinary families,' he said, after a YouGov poll found that respondents thought he wasn't up to the job of prime minister.

Segments of a political memoir *Power Trip: a decade of policy, plots and spin* written by Damian McBride, Gordon Brown's former spin doctor, had been published in the *Daily Mail* (reportedly for a fee of around £130,000) telling how he operated to bring down ministers seen as rivals to his master. The timing, on the eve of a crucial party conference for Ed Miliband, appeared designed to inflict damage, along with claims that the Labour leader could in future be embarrassed by emails he exchanged with a friend of McBride's, Derek Draper. Alastair Campbell described the actions of McBride, in allowing his book to damage Labour on the eve of conference, as 'sickening'.

Morten Morland
The Times
23 September 2013

Peter Brookes
The Times
24 September 2013

Labour's shadow chancellor Ed Balls denied having had anything to do with the 'despicable' negative briefings of the party's former spin doctor, Damian McBride, despite being close allies at the time. When asked whether he could categorically state that he was never involved in negative briefing against a government colleague, Ed Balls said, 'Yes. That's not something I've ever done, I think it's the wrong way to do politics.'

Andy Davey
The Sun
24 September 2013

According to the cartoonist: Angela Merkel preparing for her third term in office. How will history remember her? She has always been known as the hard woman of the German centre-right — all tight fiscal rules and trouser suits. However, with her yielding to Greek demands for funds at EU level, her reputation is not as clear cut as hardliners like Thatcher and Bismarck.

ANYTHING BUT CHEMICALS

The UN Security Council voted unanimously to require Syria to eliminate its arsenal of chemical weapons. The UN resolution was based on a deal struck between Obama and Putin that averted an American military intervention in Syria. Two Republican US senators criticised the resolution, saying it would do little to end the civil war. 'This is another triumph of hope over reality,' John McCain and Lindsey Graham stated. The pair also said that Assad's forces will continue to 'use every weapon in their arsenal short of chemical weapons' on the Syrian people while receiving outside assistance from Russia, Iran, and Hezbollah while doing so.

Ingram Pinn
Financial Times
28 September 2013

Peter Brookes
The Times
4 October 2013

Ed Miliband accused David Cameron of reviving memories of Margaret Thatcher's notorious description of the miners as 'the enemy within' after the latter had described the trade unions as a 'threat to the economy'.
Mia Farrow hinted that the father of her son, Ronan, may have been her ex husband, Frank Sinatra — Ol' Blue Eyes — rather than her former partner, Woody Allen. Farrow was married to Sinatra from 1966 to 1968. Their relationship continued sporadically afterwards, including during the early years of her relationship with Allen.

FINAL CURTAIN?

Ingram Pinn
Financial Times
5 October 2013

The Italian government survived a vote of confidence despite a threat by Silvio Berlusconi to bring it down. Berlusconi was forced into an abrupt change of plan after his own party colleagues rejected his demands, and supported the government. Berlusconi's demands came in anticipation of a planned vote that could have stripped him of his Senate seat, following his tax fraud conviction and a sentence of one year of house arrest or community service. The episode cast further doubt about Berlusconi's future in Italian politics.

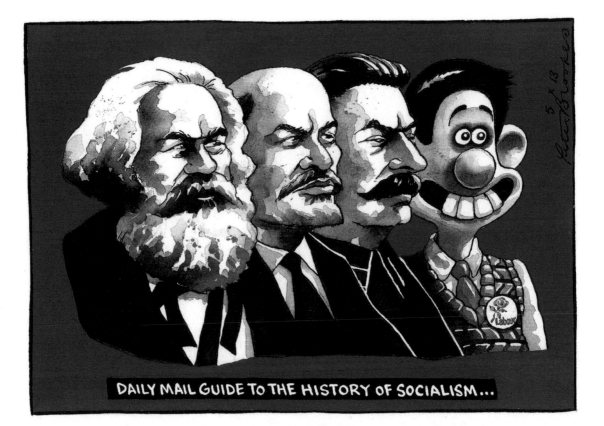

DAILY MAIL GUIDE TO THE HISTORY OF SOCIALISM...

Ed Miliband accused the *Daily Mail* of lying about his father after it headlined an article about him as 'The man who hated Britain'. The newspaper questioned how the beliefs of Ralph Miliband, a Marxist academic, may have influenced his son. The editor, Paul Dacre, referring to Ed Miliband's speech to the Labour Party conference, said the *Daily Mail* was 'deeply concerned that after all the failures of socialism in the 20th Century, the leader of the Labour Party was announcing its return, complete with land seizures and price fixing ... Our point was simply this: Ralph Miliband was, as a Marxist, committed to smashing the institutions that make Britain distinctively British. The picture that emerged was of a man who gave unqualified support to Russian totalitarianism until the mid-50s, who loathed the market economy, was in favour of a workers' revolution, denigrated British traditions and institutions such as the Royal Family, the church and the Army and was overtly dismissive of western democracy.'

Peter Brookes
The Times
5 October 2013

Dave Simonds
The Observer
6 October 2013

According to the cartoonist: David Cameron and Iain Duncan Smith find a new way to cut benefits to those who are young and vulnerable. David Cameron signalled a major overhaul in benefits for 18- to 24-year-olds when he announced plans to withdraw housing benefit and jobseeker's allowance from many of the one million youngsters currently not in work, education, or training.

Christian Adams
The Daily Telegraph
7 October 2013

David Cameron launched phase two of the 'Help to Buy' scheme, designed to help people unable to raise a big deposit to get on or move up the housing ladder, with 95 per cent mortgages backed by government guarantee. At a Cabinet meeting earlier in the year, George Osborne is said to have quipped: 'Hopefully we will get a little housing boom and everyone will be happy as property values go up.' The chancellor's joke misfired — some Cabinet colleagues felt that raising the prospect of another housing bubble was no laughing matter. Officially, the Government was playing down the threat of another housing boom, despite a rise in house prices.

Steve Bell
The Guardian
10 October 2013

According to the first skills survey by the Organisation for Economic Co-operation and Development, England is the only country in the developed world where the generation approaching retirement is more literate and numerate than the youngest adults. In a stark assessment of the success and failure of the 720-million-strong adult workforce across the wealthier economies, the economic think-tank warned that, in England, adults aged 55 to 65 perform better than 16- to 24-year-olds at foundation levels of literacy and numeracy. The OECD study also found that a quarter of adults in England have the maths skills of a 10-year-old.

Martin Rowson
The Guardian
12 October 2013

The Government's business secretary Vince Cable stated that the Royal Mail 'had to' be privatised. Royal Mail shares had risen more than 38% to 456p at the start of dealings on the London Stock Exchange. Cable also said the sell-off is 'giving [the Royal mail] a future' as it 'will now be able to compete'. He insisted, despite claims of the Royal Mail being vastly undervalued, the move was 'a very good deal' for shareholders, the country, and the government.

David Cameron has no further plans to meet the Dalai Lama, George Osborne claimed as he made it clear Britain is determined to move on from a row with Beijing over contacts with Tibet's spiritual leader. Unveiling plans to streamline visas for Chinese business leaders and tourists, the chancellor said the UK should show respect for a 'deep and ancient civilisation' as Beijing deals with its problems. The chancellor was leading a five-strong ministerial delegation to China, designed to pave the way for an official visit by the prime minister, who has not visited the country for three years. Cameron was forced to abandon a visit to China after Beijing downgraded its relations with Britain after he met the Dalai Lama in 2012.

Brian Adcock
The Independent
14 October 2013

DEBT CRISIS LATEST

REPUBLICAN H.Q.

ADAMS 15/10
after BANKSY.

Christian Adams
The Daily Telegraph
15 October 2013

After more than 10 days of stalemate in the US over the partial US government shutdown, and the raising of the nation's debt limit, President Obama agreed to talks with the Republican Speaker of the House of Representatives, John Boehner. Analysts took a positive note that talks were happening. House Majority Leader Eric Cantor said the talks were 'very useful' and 'clarifying'. Hopes were that the two sides would agree on a temporary increase to the US debt limit, as failure to do so could have dire consequences for the global economy.

Steve Bell
The Guardian
16 October 2013

A senior police officer described how evidence was doctored against Andrew Mitchell: 'On the 18 September, 2012 Mr Mitchell had insisted on being let out through the main gate. Following this [officer X] said to the other officers: "Right, we can stitch him up".' The whistleblower also stated that the word 'plebs' was added by the named officer to the original police log of the conversation that Mitchell was said to have had with the officer who was guarding the gates on 19 September.

Dave Simonds
The Observer
20 October 2013

New research showed that members of the 'big six' group of energy suppliers were paying very low or even no corporation tax, despite reaping significant profits from high domestic bills. This prompted outrage from MPs and calls for reform of the way the industry is regulated. According to the cartoonist: The 'big six' energy companies seem to concentrate their energies on amassing profits for themselves whilst hiking the bills for their customers.

Ed Miliband said he would impose a levy on the profits of payday lenders, which would, in turn, be used to double the amount of public funding for low-cost alternatives. Miliband also confirmed that Labour would impose a cap on the cost of credit, and give councils the power to stop the spread of payday lending shops in town centres. This was seen as another attempt by the Labour leader to take the side of the consumer against 'profiteering capitalism'.

Brian Adcock
The Independent
22 October 2013

Peter Schrank

The Independent on Sunday
25 October 2013

The furore over the scale of American mass surveillance revealed by Edward Snowden shifted to a new level when German chancellor Angela Merkel called President Obama to demand explanations over reports that the US National Security Agency was monitoring her mobile phone. Merkel was said to have been 'livid'.
According to the cartoonist: Shared stories, such as myths, fairytales, and the bible, can prove a useful context for cartoonists. I particularly like to put Merkel into a Grimm's fairytale setting. It's the right cultural background for her.

Christian Adams
The Daily Telegraph
28 October 2013

David Cameron revealed his deep anger at Ed Miliband's wavering stance over the £42.6 billion high-speed rail line, accusing him of playing 'petty politics' with the national interest. Tory MP Andrew Stephenson said it was 'absolutely outrageous' for Labour to be challenging the project after years of vocal support, warning the Opposition party was 'putting in jeopardy jobs and investment in the north of England'. Cameron had made it clear that the project would require support from all three main parties to proceed.

Scott Clissold
Sunday Express
3 November 2013

A new system of regulating the British press was approved — a move newspapers said was draconian and threatened freedom of speech. The development paved the way for a new industry regulator, making it easier for people who feel they have been wronged by the press to have their complaints heard, and allowing the new press watchdog to levy fines of up to 1 million pounds. All three main political parties backed the new rules.

Ben Jennings
The Guardian
4 November 2013

According to the cartoonist: The Pleb Gate debacle became so farcical that it reminded me of a performance of Punch and Judy, with Andrew Mitchell whacking the policeman once it turned out they'd tried to stitch him up. Of course, Mitchell had some rather powerful allies during this ordeal to watch his back, unlike many others who do not have that privilege when fighting an injustice.

Steve Bright 'Brighty'
The Sun
4 November 2013

A senior Conservative MP questioned the legitimacy of Ed Miliband's leadership of the Labour Party after it emerged that Britain's biggest union was facing an investigation into Unite Union's general secretary Len McCluskey's re-election. McCluskey had won with the help of 160,000 'phantom' voters who were not members of the union. Jerry Hicks, his rival for the job, complained that the ballot was unlawful, and that ballot papers were even sent to dead former members. Ed Miliband had defeated his brother, David, to become Labour leader, with the support of almost 50,000 Unite members.

NUCLEAR DEAL...

Morten Morland
The Times
9 November 2013

Israel's political establishment arose in unison to denounce as inadequate an interim agreement hammered out with Iran to rein in its nuclear programme. Benjamin Netanyahu led the chorus of indignation, calling the deal struck in Geneva between Iran and the US, Britain, France, Russia, China, and Germany 'a historic mistake'. Netanyahu's comments came after a procession of Israeli ministers and senior officials had earlier taken aim at a 'bad deal' which they said effectively left Iran as a nuclear threshold state.

Steve Bell
The Guardian
12 November 2013

Former prime minister Sir John Major said the influence that the privately educated, middle-class elite have had on public life was 'shocking', while he blamed 'the collapse in social mobility' on the failures of the last Labour government.

Morten Morland
The Times
14 November 2013

There is no room for complacency despite the 'welcome' return to economic growth, Ed Balls, the shadow chancellor, told the CBI Annual Conference. 'The return to growth is something to celebrate and nurture,' he told delegates. 'But with business investment still on hold and banking lending to small business still falling, with youth unemployment still very high, with living standards still falling for most people this is no time for complacency.'

NO GRAVITAS

Brian Adcock
The Independent
17 November 2013

Labour forged an eight-point lead over the Conservatives, the biggest since March, in a *Guardian*/ICM poll. The poll also showed that the party leader, Ed Miliband, was outperforming David Cameron on several personal scores but not on the crucial question of who makes the best prime minister.

Christian Adams
The Daily Telegraph
19 November 2013

As President Barack Obama's approval rating hit another all-time low, a new national survey indicated that Americans believed the president had less power than congressional Republicans when it came to shaping future events.

David Cameron promised an inquiry into how The Co-operative Bank had been 'driven into the wall' by former chairman Paul Flowers, and asked why alarm bells over his behaviour hadn't rung earlier. Flowers, a one-time local Labour politician with no banking qualifications, oversaw the co-op's near-collapse during his tenure as chairman. A video of him allegedly arranging to buy illegal drugs had been exposed by a newspaper. Cameron accused the opposition Labour Party, of which Flowers was a member and a backer, of knowing about Flowers' behaviour.

Steve Bell
The Guardian
21 November 2013

Morten Morland
The Times
21 November 2013

Defence Secretary Philip Hammond fought off a Tory rebellion over the Government's controversial Army reorganisation, after making last-minute concessions. The Conservative amendment, which could have delayed plans to expand the Army Reserve to 30,000 to offset cuts of 20,000 in regular forces by 2020, was defeated by 306 votes to 252.

HUG A HUSKY...

22 XI 13

Peter Brookes

Peter Brookes
The Times
22 November 2013

David Cameron ordered ministers to ditch the 'green crap' blamed for driving up energy bills and making business uncompetitive. The prime minister, who once pledged to lead the 'greenest government ever', has publicly promised to 'roll back' green taxes, which add more than £110 a year to average fuel bills. Back in 2006, Cameron wanted to help save the planet. He even hugged a husky when the WWF took him to the Arctic and showed him the damaging effects of climate change.

Chris Riddell
The Observer
24 November 2013

During Prime Minister's Questions, Ed Miliband claimed that David Cameron had reached a 'new low' by using the Co-op Bank's near collapse and its former chairman's high-profile troubles to score political points. In a strongly-worded attack on the Tory leadership's style, Miliband accused the Prime Minister of resorting to a strategy of mud-slinging in an effort to win the 2015 election.

Steve Bright 'Brighty'
The Sun
24 November 2013

Ed Miliband appeared on Radio 4's 'Desert Island Discs'. Robbie Williams, A-ha, and Neil Diamond were some of the artists on his playlist. Defending his picks, Miliband said that his music taste may not be 'cool' but he did at least pick his own songs. When David Cameron had appeared on the radio show in 2006, and cited bands like The Smiths and Radiohead, he was accused of letting spin doctors put the list together to make him look more credible. Miliband, however, insisted his choices were entirely his own.

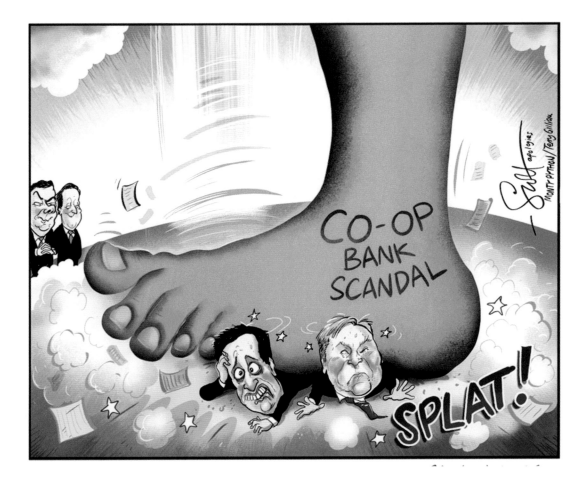

Scott Clissold
Sunday Express
24 November 2013

Labour was plunged into a financial crisis in the wake of The Co-operative Bank scandal. More than £2 million in loans from the co-op and a sister bank had been secured by Labour Party officials on favourable terms in April. Labour now faced the prospect of having to pay off the loans early — and before the 2015 general election — as the bank had a £1.5 billion black hole in its finances. The surviving members of Monty Python had announced they would star in a revival at London's O2 arena.

Bob Moran
The Daily Telegraph
29 November 2013

According to the cartoonist: T-shirts with writing on them, if used sparingly, can be a useful comedy tool. It was also a good way of depicting the traditional 'doublespeak' of Boris Johnson.

Dave Brown
The Independent
3 December 2013

Responding to accusations that he is more like a businessman and less like a politician, during a trade visit to China, David Cameron said, 'We have got to get out there and bat for Britain.' Cameron tweeted that his China trade visit had led to £5.6 billion in business deals.

Morten Morland
The Times
3 December 2013

David Cameron was forced to protest directly to the Chinese President, Xi Jinping, after a British journalist was barred from attending a press conference in Beijing with the country's premier. However, President Xi said he knew nothing about the subject when the prime minister raised the matter, and refused to act on British concerns over the press event, where questions had not been permitted.

Peter Schrank
The Independent on Sunday
8 December 2013

South Africa's first black president and anti-apartheid icon Nelson Mandela died at the age of 95. Mandela had led South Africa's transition from white-minority rule in the 1990s, after 27 years in prison for his political activities. Announcing the news on South African national TV, President Jacob Zuma said that Mandela was 'now at peace'.

Martin Rowson
The Guardian
9 December 2013

Plans to award MPs an 11% pay rise were criticised across Westminster, with one minister describing them as 'wholly inappropriate'. Parliamentary watchdog IPSA is set to recommend a rise of £7,600 to £74,000, to come in after the 2015 election.

Steve Bell
The Guardian
11 December 2013

At the memorial service for Nelson Mandela, a grinning David Cameron and Barack Obama posed for a 'selfie' with Danish prime minister Helle Thorning-Schmidt as she took the snap on her camera phone. Within minutes the photograph of the three leaders posing for the 'selfie' went viral on the internet, staking its claim to become the most famous, if controversial, taken so far.

Peter Brookes
The Times
17 December 2013

David Cameron boldly declared that Britain's mission will be 'accomplished' in Afghanistan by the time troops pull out next year. His remarks risked comparisons with the notorious 'Mission Accomplished' speech given by former US president George W. Bush about Iraq, in May 2003, after Saddam Hussein's regime had been overthrown, only for an insurgency to take hold, which claimed thousands of lives.

Kevin Kallaugher 'KAL'
The Economist
18 December 2013

Conservative critics in America attacked Pope Francis, after he had suggested that huge salaries and bonuses were symptoms of an economy based on greed and inequality. After American radio talk-show host Rush Limbaugh had, as a result, called him a marxist, the Pope responded by saying that he was not a Marxist, but that even Marxists could be good people.

Paul Thomas
Daily Express
19 December 2013

David Cameron stated that it was likely that his government would not meet its target of reducing net immigration to the UK to 'tens of thousands' by 2015. The latest immigration figures showed that immigration in the year to June 2013 rose by 15,000 to 182,000. After 31st December 2013, restrictions on Romanians working within the EU would expire.

Chris Riddell
The Observer
22 December 2013

David Cameron revealed he had been keeping a 'little black book' of Tory ideas he claimed the Lib Dems had stopped him doing in government. Cameron will put them in the next Tory manifesto in the hope he can return to Downing Street at the next election without again being in coalition with the Lib Dems. The Tory election plan envisages a route to a parliamentary majority by decapitating 20 Lib Dem MPs.

SCROOGED...

YOU THERE BOY! RUN TO THE FOODBANK AND FETCH ME THEIR LARGEST PACKET OF SAGE + ONION... ...I'M GOING TO STUFF TINY TIM!

Dave Brown
The Independent
24 December 2013

Iain Duncan Smith, the embattled work and pensions secretary, refused to meet leaders of the rapidly expanding Christian charity that had set up more than 400 food banks across the UK, claiming it was 'scaremongering' and had a clear political agenda. The news fuelled a growing row over food poverty, as church leaders and the Labour party accused ministers of failing to recognise the growing crisis hitting hundreds of thousands of families whose incomes were squeezed, while food prices soared.

Ben Jennings
The Guardian
30 December 2013

According to the cartoonist: With people plunging further and further into debt, the Bank of England's decision to raise interest rates in the near future could prove catastrophic for many.

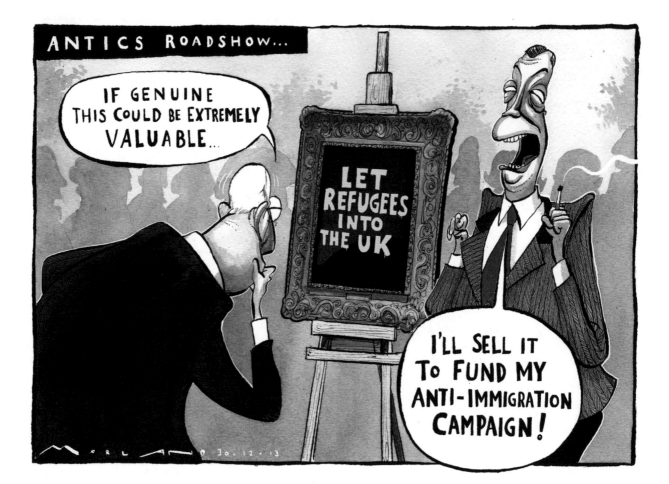

Morten Morland
The Times
30 December 2013

UKIP leader Nigel Farage said that the UK should take in some of the refugees from Syria's civil war. Farage, who had led opposition to allowing open immigration from Romania and Bulgaria, said refugees were 'a very different thing to economic migration'.

31 · 12 · 13

Morten Morland
The Times
31 December 2013

At least 14 people were killed in a suicide bombing on a trolleybus in the Russian city of Volgograd. The blast came a day after 17 people died in another suicide attack at the central station in the city. Moscow was concerned that militants could be ramping up violence in the run-up to the 2014 Winter Olympic Games in the city of Sochi in February. The Olympics venue is close to the troubled republics of Chechnya and Dagestan.

According to the cartoonist: During the coalition's tenure one of the most prominent issues has been immigration, with the rise of UKIP pushing rhetoric from all parties to the right on this issue. Towards the end of 2013 there was a particular frenzy in politics and the media about the flood gates apparently opening on the 1st January to a large number of Bulgarians and Romanians, once certain EU restrictions had been lifted, as prophesied by Nigel Farage (29 million people I believe was the UKIP estimate, more than the population of both countries combined). This turned out to be a bit of an anti-climax, but in the run-up all sorts of anti-immigrant sentiment was being spouted by the government to try and quell people's fears being exacerbated by UKIP, such as the infamous 'Go Home' vans. This particular cartoon was focusing on a policy floated around by the Coalition that EU migrants would have to pay to access A&E to try and stop so called 'Health Tourism'.

Ben Jennings
The Guardian
31 December 2013

Dave Brown
The Independent
2 January 2014

North Korean leader Kim Jong-un hailed the elimination of 'factional filth' following the execution of his uncle in December. During his New Year message, which was broadcast on state television, Kim said: 'Our party took resolute action to remove ... scum elements within the party last year.' He accused his uncle Jang Song-thaek, who was previously considered the second most powerful man in the secretive state, of committing treason.

Peter Brookes
The Times
3 January 2014

In what was seen as an effort to win back voters from UKIP, David Cameron vowed to control immigration, as restrictions on the free movement of workers from Bulgaria and Romania were lifted throughout the whole of the EU. Meanwhile, authorities in both Sofia and Bucharest said the UK's fear of a large number of arrivals was unfounded. People who wanted to leave and find work in the UK had already done so.

Bob Moran
The Daily Telegraph
3 January 2014

According to the cartoonist: It's nice when two stories can be bundled together neatly as happened here.
This is an unusually personal cartoon in that I was commuting by train and hoping to buy a house at the time.
Both seemed like impossible dreams.

"WELL, IF YOU KNOWS OF A BIGGER ****'OLE, GO TO 'IM!"

Martin Rowson
The Guardian
6 January 2014

Michael Gove claimed left-wing myths about the World War I peddled by 'Blackadder' belittled Britain and cleared Germany of blame. The education secretary criticised historians and TV programmes that denigrate patriotism and courage by depicting the war as a 'misbegotten shambles'. In an article for the *Daily Mail*, Gove said he had little time for the view that the commemorations should not lay fault at Germany's door. Gove stated the conflict was a 'just war' to combat aggression by a German elite bent on domination.

CONTINUED FLOODS...

THE ASHES

6·1·14

Morten Morland
The Times
6 January 2014

Stormy weather continued to wreak havoc into January. A combination of high winds, rain, and strong waves battered the coastline and also caused flooding further inland. On the third and final day of the fifth Test against England, Australia completed only the third whitewash in the history of the Ashes.

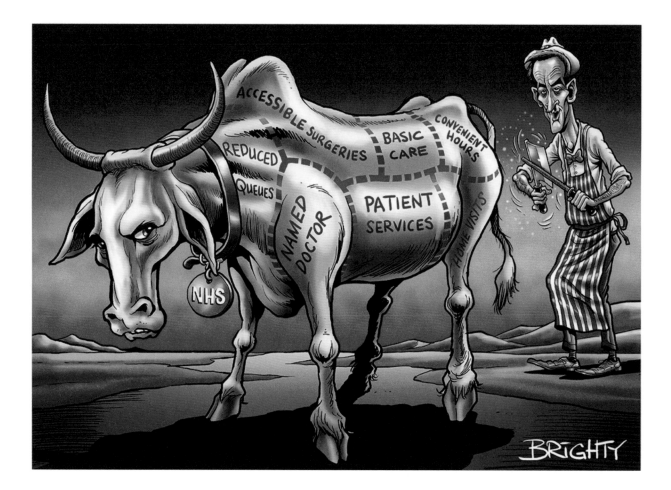

Steve Bright 'Brighty'
The Sun
6 January 2014

The health service was making the biggest cost savings in its history, in a £20 billion 'efficiency programme' that health minister Jeremy Hunt said was designed to cut costs of existing care but which critics claimed was leading to cuts in services.

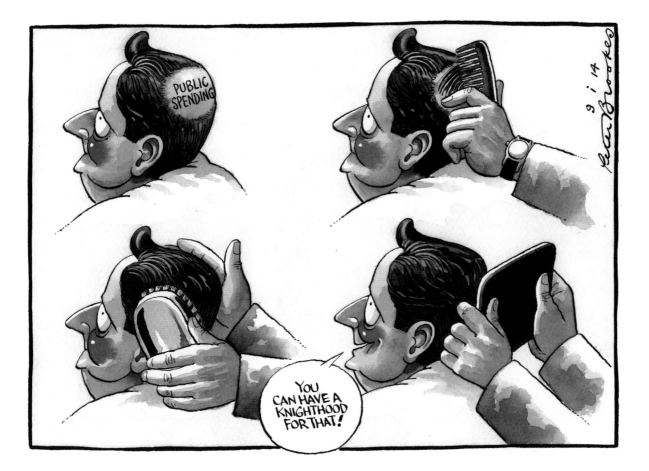

Peter Brookes
The Times
9 January 2014

David Cameron, who entered office with thick, dark hair, had recently taken to having it brushed back and carefully positioned to cover a thinning crown. Lino Carbosiero, the prime minister's barber, who was awarded an MBE in the New Year's Honours, displayed the utmost tact when questioned about the prime minister's bald spot; Carbosiero laughed and replied: 'What bald spot?'

Bob Moran
The Daily Telegraph
11 January 2014

According to the cartoonist: I think this was quite a late idea. Trying to do a cartoon about police corruption without being dark and depressing or highly insensitive was proving tricky. At first, this seemed too obvious, but I think that's what made it funny.

Steve Bell
The Guardian
14 January 2014

David Cameron declared that his government was 'going all out for shale' as he announced that councils would be entitled to keep 100 per cent of business rates raised from fracking sites, in a deal expected to generate millions of pounds for local authorities. The prime minister's announcement, likened to a bribe by environmentalists, came on the day that the French energy group Total became the first global oil company to invest in a shale gas exploration project in Britain.

Peter Brookes
The Times
15 January 2014

At a press conference to launch policies to help France's struggling economy, François Hollande declined to comment on claims that he had been having an affair with an actress, saying that it was neither the time nor the place to discuss it. The French president instead outlined his plans to work with bosses to reduce unemployment and cut state spending.

According to the cartoonist: This cartoon was illustrating a piece on the various factions trying to obstruct an improvement in relations between Iran and the US. I tried to show that Obama had to overcome resistance from within the House of Congress, from, amongst others, Jewish and pro-Israeli lobby groups. Using the Star of David (especially as different from the flag of Israel) as a label can touch on a sensitive nerve, especially if there is a suggestion of hidden influence, or even conspiracy. Accordingly there was a strong reaction from mainly American pressure groups and individuals, some of it very abusive and threatening towards *The Economist* and myself. *The Economist* was quick to disassociate itself from the cartoon, removing it from their website and printing an apology in the following issue.

Peter Schrank
The Economist
18 January 2014

OSBORNE WARNS EU

Ingram Pinn
Financial Times
18 January 2014

George Osborne claimed that Britain's status as a free-market nation was at risk from 'the forces of pessimism' who were waging war on big business. An anti-business alliance of Labour and the 'populist Right' (a reference to UKIP) want to 'pull up the drawbridge and shut Britain off from the world', the chancellor said. Osborne's remarks were designed as a provocative riposte to those in his own party and UKIP who have expressed concern about foreign take-overs, most recently the stalled Pfizer bid for British-based drugs firm AstraZeneca.

Peter Schrank
The Independent on Sunday
19 January 2014

Ed Miliband likened the 'broken' banking system to the energy market, claiming 'too much power is concentrated in too few hands'. Under Labour, Miliband said, 'instead of you serving the banks, the banks will serve you'. The 'big five' banks HSBC, Barclays, RBS, Santander, and Lloyds Banking Group account for the majority of bank customers and lending. According to the cartoonist: Clichés, such as 'tilting at windmills', are a useful tool for cartoonists, particularly in a wordless cartoon. If the cliché is tired and overused it can fall flat, unless given a fresh twist. Looking at it now I'm bothered by a slightly dodgy perspective on the windmill's wings.

'Oh come on, mother. How are you going to prove Lloyd George pinched your bottom?'

Stan McMurtry 'Mac'
Daily Mail
21 January 2014

Liberal Democrat peer Lord Rennard was suspended from the Lib Dem party after declining to apologise over sexual harassment claims. Lord Rennard insisted he had not done anything wrong, and wanted to resume his seat in the House of Lords. Lib Dem MP Lynne Featherstone told the BBC: 'An apology is the very least that should be delivered ... As a Liberal Democrat and as a woman, I wish he had apologised.'

© Steve Bell 2014 – 3614·22·1·14·   ·WITH APOLOGIES·

Steve Bell
The Guardian
22 January 2014

The United States expressed horror at an enormous cache of photographs documenting how the Syrian regime had killed an estimated 11,000 detainees, warning that the evidence of war crimes had cast a shadow over imminent peace talks. An inquiry by three former prosecutors, who reviewed some 55,000 images smuggled out of the country, revealed the 'systematic torture and killing' of prisoners held by Bashar al-Assad's forces.

Christian Adams
The Daily Telegraph
24 January 2013

After numerous lacklustre performances in the Commons by his shadow chancellor, Ed Miliband refused to pledge that Ed Balls would be chancellor if Labour won the next election. The Work and Pensions Committee concluded that Jobcentre Plus should continue to provide a public employment service for the unemployed.

Chris Riddell
The Observer
2 February 2014

David Cameron faced a fresh clash with Tory Eurosceptics after dropping Britain's objections to the use of the European court of justice to enforce a new fiscal compact for the eurozone. Cameron did, however, pledge to watch eurozone leaders 'like a hawk' and to take legal action if they attempted to use the court, or any other EU institution, to rewrite the rules of the single market.

Peter Brookes
The Times
5 February 2014

An Ipsos MORI poll found that four in ten trusted David Cameron more than the other party leaders to deal with managing the economy, compared to 20% trusting Ed Miliband, 5% Clegg and 3% Farage.

Dave Brown
The Independent
5 February 2014

Prince Charles visited flood-hit villages that had been cut off by the wettest January for more than a century. The heir to the throne met residents, farmers, and emergency staff in the stricken county of Somerset. Charles pledged £50,000 from his Prince's Countryside Fund to help the region. His visit came as David Cameron faced anger over his response to the floods.

'Well honestly. Last year it was leaves on the line. What's the excuse this time?'

Stan McMurtry 'Mac'
Daily Mail
6 February 2014

Rail services in the south-west were cut off from the rest of the county after a section of seawall under a coastal railway line collapsed. The seawall at Dawlish, Devon, collapsed after heavy storms, demolishing part of the railway line.

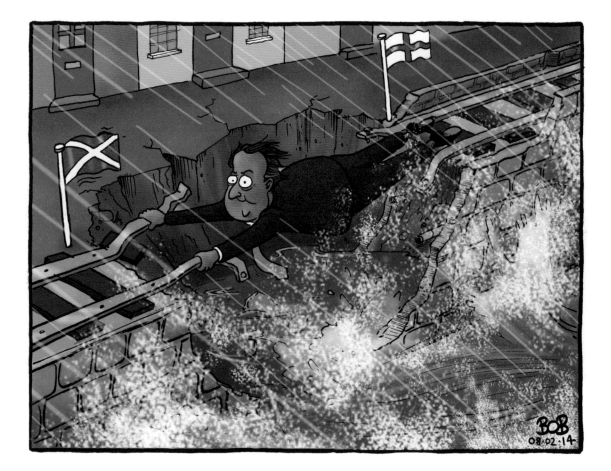

Bob Moran
The Daily Telegraph
8 February 2014

According to the cartoonist: Extreme weather (for the UK) dominating headlines can be annoying as there isn't much to say beyond 'everyone's wet'. However, Cameron made a speech on Scottish independence and then travelled to Dawlish to see the broken railway line on the same day. As far as cartoon material goes, you'd have to call it a perfect storm (sorry).

Chris Riddell
The Observer
9 February 2014

The lead-up to the Winter Olympics in Russia was overshadowed by the Putin regime's tough anti-gay laws and the rise of extreme homophobia in the country. Russia had enacted laws criminalising 'gay propaganda' and lesbian, gay, bisexual, and transgender rights activists had been attacked in the streets.

Ben Jennings
The Guardian
10 February 2014

According to the cartoonist: Nick Clegg suggested reforming drug laws due to the failure of prohibition. Whilst the debate on the legality of drugs is certainly one worth having, I saw this as a rather cynical ploy by Clegg to try and appear hip again and separate himself from the Tories, as he did in the run-up to the 2010 general election to many young voters, before shacking up in a coalition with the Tories and committing political suicide by allowing tuition fees to be trebled, rather than abolished as he had promised his following.

Peter Brookes
The Times
12 February 2014

David Cameron assured voters he was taking control of the flooding emergency, with a rare press conference in Downing Street in which he pledged that 'money is no object' for flood repair operations. 'We are a wealthy country, we have a growing economy, we've taken good care of our public finances,' Cameron told reporters. 'In recovering from these floods, money is no object.'

Steve Bell
The Guardian
13 February 2014

George Osborne came under increasing pressure to use his next Budget to increase Government spending on flood defences. He rejected claims that budget cuts were to blame for the cutback in dredging, which many said was responsible for widespread flooding across Somerset. Osborne also said a vote for Scottish independence would result in the Scots walking away from the pound.

Scott Clissold
Sunday Express
15 February 2014

The Scottish National Party came under pressure to set out an alternative to a formal currency union with the rest of the UK in the event of independence, after the three main unionist parties said they would not agree to such a deal. SNP leader Alex Salmond said the joint move by the Conservatives, Labour, and Liberal Democrats was 'a concerted bid by a Tory-led Westminster establishment to bully and intimidate'.

Steve Bright 'Brighty'
The Sun
17 February 2014

Had Labour elected its leader by one person, one vote, David, the winner among party members and MPs, would have taken the crown. Ed stole it because his backers among the big unions helped tilt the playing field in his favour, by giving his team access to their membership lists while withholding them from his rivals. Some unions even accompanied the ballot paper with 'Vote Ed' literature, which is like going to the polling station at general election time and finding a 'Vote Conservative' or 'Vote Labour' leaflet inside the ballot paper.

Building [Suspension - of Disbelief] Bridges...

18·2·14

Martin Rowson
The Guardian
18 February 2014

Nick Clegg fuelled speculation that he was positioning for coalition with Labour after the next election by saying he believed Ed Miliband's party had 'changed'. Clegg, at the same time, criticised the Tories for lurching to the right. These comments followed an apparent thaw in relations with shadow chancellor Ed Balls. The animosity between the men had previously been regarded as a major obstacle to the two parties joining up if there is a hung parliament after next May's general election.

Kevin Kallaugher 'KAL'
The Economist
19 February 2014

China rejected a UN report accusing North Korea of crimes against humanity, brushing it off as 'unreasonable criticism'. The report was an unprecedented indictment of the isolated country's leaders, highlighting widespread rape, torture, forced abortions, and other atrocities in its network of forced labour camps. It recommended that North Korean officials, possibly including its 31-year-old leader Kim Jong-un, be tried before the International Criminal Court.

THE GREAT **EU** DEBATE

BOB
22·02·14

Bob Moran
The Daily Telegraph
22 February 2014

According to the cartoonist: This was a gentle comment on the overall insignificance of the debate between Nigel Farage and Nick Clegg. I was also aware of how many Telegraph readers would nevertheless be hoping for Nige to give Nick a ruddy good kicking. Mr Farage sent me a nice email about it and promised to send me a bottle of whiskey. It still hasn't arrived...

Steve Bright 'Brighty'
The Sun
23 February 2014

During the 2014 Russian Winter Olympic Games in Sochi, Moscow was accused by the West of orchestrating a 'military invasion and occupation' of the Crimean peninsula, as groups of apparently pro-Russian armed men seized control of two airports. Russian troop movements were reported across the territory. One Ukrainian official claimed that 2,000 Russian troops had arrived in Crimea during the course of the day, in 13 Russian aircrafts.

Boris Johnson hit out at the RMT union boss Bob Crow after pictures emerged of him sunning himself on a Brazilian beach just days before the first 48-hour tube strike. Johnson said, while he did not begrudge Mr Crow his holiday, he was not entitled to disrupt the lives of millions of people trying to go about their everyday business: 'I love a beach holiday myself; like Bob, I have some groovy swimwear that doesn't always meet with acclaim; and I consider it the right of every freeborn Englishman to drink a bottle of wine and turn the colour of a lobster in the sun. Bob Crow is entitled to his holiday.'

Christian Adams
The Daily Telegraph
26 February 2014

An investigation by the GMB union found that landlords were receiving the majority of the £23 billion of taxpayers' money that went towards subsidising the rent for 1.65 million private properties in the UK. The top 20 company landlords in each of the 311, out of 380, councils receive housing benefit direct from councils for tenants renting their properties. The list of the companies' owners and directors included two viscounts, two dukes, five earls, three marquises, a marquess, four barons, a baroness, and a knight. At least 10 of the landlords own castles, and were receiving upwards of £10,000 a year in housing benefit.

Robert Amos
Morning Star
1 March 2014

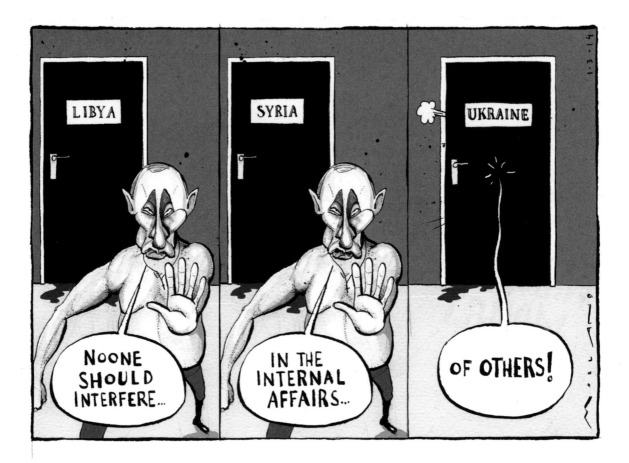

Morten Morland
The Times
1 March 2014

Acting Ukrainian president Oleksander Turchynov called on Vladimir Putin to withdraw troops from Crimea. In a TV address, he appealed to Moscow to 'immediately stop provoking us'. It came amid reports that Russian planes had flown hundreds of troops into the region.

Steve Bright 'Brighty'
The Sun
3 March 2014

Harriet Harman had said she 'regrets' a civil liberties group she once worked for had links to pro-paedophile campaigners in the 1970s, but insisted she had 'nothing to apologise for'. The National Council for Civil Liberties granted 'affiliate' status to the Paedophile Information Exchange. The *Daily Mail* had urged the deputy Labour leader to explain this link. But Harman accused the newspaper of 'smear and innuendo' and said it 'should be apologising'. From 1978 to 1982 Ms Harman was legal officer at the National Council for Civil Liberties, which was the predecessor to the campaign group Liberty.

The Great Debate

Martin Rowson
The Guardian
6 March 2014

Nigel Farage hit out at Nick Clegg for being a 'hypocrite' after the Deputy Prime Minister suggested the UKIP leader and his MEPs were lazy and ineffective. Clegg had accused Farage of being 'happy' to take their European parliament salaries while 'rarely' turning up for votes. Rowson drew Clegg as Pinocchio, the 'little wooden boy who wants to become a real politician'.

RESURFACING...

Dave Brown
The Independent
11 March 2014

Gordon Brown made his first intervention in the Scottish independence debate by calling for a better power-sharing deal with Westminster. The former prime minister said that there should be a bill of rights clearly setting out the arrangements between Scotland and the UK parliaments. Speaking in Glasgow, Brown said, 'The majority of Scottish people do not want separation but equally they do want change, not the status quo.'

Kevin Kallaugher 'KAL'
The Economist
13 March 2014

Just two weeks after Russia's military seized control of Crimea, Russian state media claimed that Crimeans voted overwhelmingly to break with Ukraine and join Russia. According to the head of the referendum commission, 95.5% had chosen the option of annexation by Moscow. Turnout was 83%, he added — a high figure given that many who opposed the move had said they would boycott the vote. Western leaders denounced the referendum as a sham.

'This letter to Miliband about a referendum. Do you want all the effing, blinding and beheading threats left in?'

Stan McMurtry 'Mac'
Daily Mail
13 March 2014

The attorney general's refusal to let the public see letters the Prince of Wales had written to ministers was ruled unlawful by the Court of Appeal. A journalist from the *Guardian* had challenged Dominic Grieve's decision to veto a High Court tribunal ruling in favour of allowing their publication. In September 2012 the Upper Tribunal, headed by a High Court judge, ruled that the public were entitled to see the letters under the Freedom of Information Act.

FOR THE WELL-BEHAVED MONKEYS

Steve Bell
The Guardian
14 March 2014

The government rejected proposals to increase NHS staff pay by 1% and will instead impose a two-year deal in which staff who receive incremental pay awards get no further rises at all. Health minister Jeremy Hunt confirmed there was no money to give nurses a pay rise.

Burial at Sea

BOB TONY

This Satirical trope is jointly operated by: SERCO, CAPITA, G4S & VIRGIN
KEEP OUT
Everybody will be prosecuted!

Martin Rowson
The Guardian
15 March 2014

The death of Bob Crow and Tony Benn within three days of each other was marked by a deluge of crocodile tears by both the media and high-ranking Conservatives. Boris Johnson, who had recently called Crow 'demented' and refused to talk to him, then heaped praise on him as a 'fighter and a man of character' after news broke of his death. Tony Benn, once referred to as the enemy within, also received glowing media tributes from his enemies and opponents. The BBC even described David Cameron as 'leading' tributes to Benn, whom he described as 'magnificent'.

Steve Bell
The Guardian
19 March 2014

The chancellor confirmed plans to extend a childcare tax break for all working families to £2,000 per child ahead of his Budget statement. The new scheme will now apply to all children under the age of 12. This cartoon is reminiscent of the memorable photograph of the extremely young and shy Diana in a see through skirt when she worked as an assistant at the Young England Kindergarten, a nursery school and day-care centre in Pimlico.

Scott Clissold
Sunday Express
23 March 2014

George Osborne caught Britain's pensions industry by surprise when he said he would scrap a rule forcing many people to buy an annuity, a financial product which converts a retiree's pension pot into a guaranteed income. From April, people would also face much less of a tax penalty if they accessed their pension savings early, at the age of 55.

Morten Morland
The Times
23 March 2014

Labour ministers appealed for calm after two dire polls led to backbench MPs openly criticising Ed Miliband for his failure to get through to voters. There were also complaints about Miliband's lacklustre response to the Budget. One senior Labour MP said, 'Our real problem is that we haven't got a strong economic message, which makes it very difficult to have a clear response to the Budget. We have got to give people a clearer idea of what our strategy will be.'

THE GREAT ESCAPE...

Dave Brown
The Independent
25 March 2014

Ed Miliband's leadership strategy came under fire from across the Labour ranks, amid rising panic that the party is drifting. A coalition of Labour grandees united in a plea for him to be more bold and clearer about his plans. In a letter to *The Guardian* they said Labour needed a mandate for 'transformative change' and warned: 'If Labour plays the next election safe, hoping to win on the basis of Tory unpopularity, it will not have earned a mandate for such change.'

Morten Morland

The Times
31 March 2014

At midnight on 28 March, gay marriage became legalised in England and Wales.
Same sex couples who wanted to have a wedding, not a civil partnership, can now have one.

Brian Adcock
Independent
31 March 2014

Debate over Scottish independence was dominated by reports that an unnamed UK minister believed that there would be a currency union after separation, in return for keeping Trident nuclear weapons at Faslane. Alex Salmond said that this showed a 'very important demolition' of Westminster's argument which would have 'severe' political consequences.

THE DEAL ...

Dave Brown
The Independent
2 April 2014

Royal Mail shares had soared more than 70%, since their stock market debut at 330p a share in October. The audit office accused the government of ignoring repeated warnings from City analysts that its plan to float Royal Mail at a maximum price of 330p a share vastly undervalued the company. According to the cartoonist: Vince Cable attempts to defend the privatisation of Royal Mail in the face of a National Audit Office report claiming the sell-off had lost the taxpayer £750m.

Ben Jennings
i newspaper
3 April 2014

According to the cartoonist: Having never been a fan of Clarkson, I relished this opportunity to mock him after a video was leaked of him saying the 'N' word on the set of *Top Gear* whilst reciting a rather bigoted version of the children's counting rhyme, 'Eeny meeny miny mo'. Clarkson arguably exacerbated the issue with his obscure apology video posted on Twitter, where he claimed he'd tried his best not to say the word. I couldn't understand how hard it was to leave out such a toxic word that I personally had never known to be included in the rhyme.

Dave Brown
The Independent
4 April 2014

Maria Miller was the first serving minister to be forced to apologise for her misuse of expenses. The expenses watchdog criticised her for claiming more than £90,000 in taxpayers' funds on a second home lived in by her parents. According to the cartoonist: David Cameron keeps faith, temporarily, with embattled culture secretary Maria Miller as the expenses scandal rears its head again. However within a few days she was a goner.

THE ROAD TO PEACE

Ingram Pinn
Financial Times
5 April 2014

Israeli-Palestinian negotiations, instigated by US Secretary of State John Kerry, resumed with the aim of ending a decades-old conflict and establishing a Palestinian state in the West Bank and Gaza Strip, with East Jerusalem as its capital, alongside Israel. However, Netanyahu was accusing Abbas of making unacceptable demands, whilst Abbas claimed Israel should commit itself to freezing settlement activity on occupied land and focus on demarcating the borders of a future Palestine.

Banquet

Martin Rowson
The Guardian
9 April 2014

Amid regal pomp at Windsor Castle, Michael D. Higgins, the Irish president and British monarch, had begun Ireland's first state visit to Britain. Martin McGuinness, a former commander of the IRA and now Northern Ireland's deputy first minister, stood for the national anthem and toasted the 'health and happiness' of the Queen at her state banquet, in a symbolically significant act for British–Irish relations.

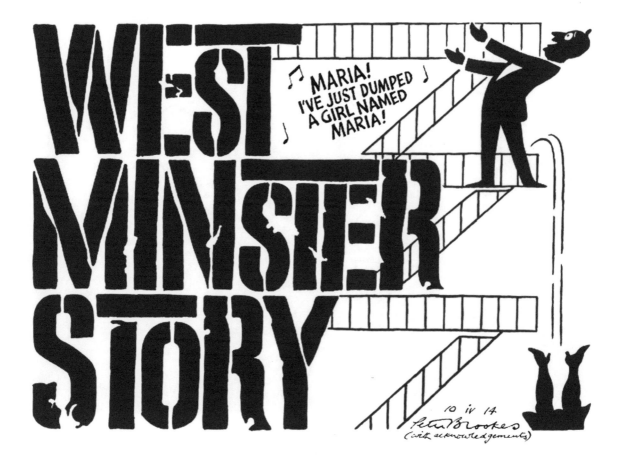

Peter Brookes
The Times
10 April 2014

David Cameron finally accepted Maria Miller's resignation as culture secretary, following a row over her expenses. The Basingstoke MP, who had apologised the previous week amid growing calls for her resignation, said the controversy had become a 'distraction from the vital work this government is doing'.

Dave Brown
The Independent
11 April 2014

There was now no full member of the Cabinet speaking for women, following the resignation of Maria Miller. The Government was being accused of being 'out of touch' when it comes to women's issues. As well as being culture secretary, Miller also oversaw the women and equalities brief. Labour's shadow minister for women and equalities Gloria De Piero said, 'David Cameron's decision to replace Maria Miller with Sajid Javid means there is now no full member of the Cabinet speaking for women. 'When it comes to women, it's "out of sight, out of mind" for this out-of-touch Government.'

Peter Brookes
The Times
11 April 2014

The acquittal of Nigel Evans on sexual assault charges, just a day after Nicholas Jacobs was acquitted of murdering PC Keith Blakelock in 1985, made it a bad week for the Crown Prosecution Service (CPS). Evans was only the latest in a series of high-profile defendants to be found not guilty of sexual assault. Inevitably, questions were being asked about why the CPS brought charges in the first place.

HOIST BY HIS OWN PETARD...

Peter Brookes
The Times
15 April 2014

Nigel Farage faced an expenses investigation into almost £60,000 of 'missing' European Union funds paid into his personal bank account. The UKIP leader had received £15,500 a year from the EU since at least 2009 to pay for the upkeep of his constituency office, but it emerged that he pays no rent because the property was gifted to him by supporters. Farage said the allegations were a 'political smear of the worst kind'.

Brian Adcock
The Independent
21 April 2014

David Cameron faced criticism from the British Humanist Association for arguing, in a *Church Times* article, that 'we should be more confident about our status as a Christian country'. According to the cartoonist: When a group of 50 signatories wrote a letter to *The Daily Telegraph* to object to David Cameron's characterisation of Britain as a 'Christian country' it partly inspired me to draw this cartoon, but the main reason was it was a good excuse to draw my fellow cartoonist Martin Rowson.

Brian Adcock
The Independent
23 April 2014

According to the cartoonist: I felt a tad sorry for David Moyes getting the boot from Manchester United but he never seemed like the right choice in the first place. The more cynical side of me might think Sir Alex Ferguson, who had a large part in choosing Moyes, might not have wanted his successor to be too impressive.

Bob Moran
The Daily Telegraph
26 April 2014

According to the cartoonist: The way to get a cartoon of The Queen past the editors is to ensure that the joke is never at Her Majesty's expense. Fortunately for this idea, the opposite rule applies where Nick Clegg is concerned.

Martin Rowson
The Guardian
26 April 2014

The Royal Bank of Scotland was blocked by the Government from asking shareholders for permission to pay bonuses twice the size of salaries in order to sidestep EU rules. The Treasury, which holds an 81% stake in the RBS, insisted the bank should remain a 'back-marker' on pay, even though other institutions would be able to ask their shareholders to approve the award of such bonus deals.

Andy Davey
The Sun
27 April 2014

A UKIP candidate sparked fresh controversy for his party after remarks he made about the comedian Lenny Henry. William Henwood, who was standing in local elections in north London, also made anti-Islamic comments. According to the cartoonist: In the run-up to the local and EU elections, several fruitcakes and weirdos emerged from the UKIP woodwork. What does go on in those selection committees? Do they actually check up on these nutjobs before nomination?

Paul Thomas
Daily Express
28 April 2014

This cartoon mirrors the *Daily Express*'s obsession with Europe and immigration, which, according to the paper, are to blame for every ill in the UK. It was announced that the classic comedy *Dad's Army* was to be made into a new feature film. *Hunger Games* actor Toby Jones will star as Arthur Lowe's iconic Captain George Mainwaring, with *Love Actually*'s Bill Nighy as Sergeant Arthur Wilson, made famous by John Le Mesurier.

MAX CLIFFORD'S FALL FROM GRACE...

Morten Morland
The Times
29 April 2014

The celebrity publicist Max Clifford was found guilty of eight indecent assaults on women and girls as young as 15 at Southwark Crown Court. He was sentenced to eight years in prison. Reports say he turned off his phone, removed his hearing loop, and turned to smile and wave at colleagues before he was taken down to the cells.

Christian Adams
The Daily Telegraph
1 May 2014

Nigel Farage announced he would not stand in the Newark by-election, saying his candidature would be a distraction. Faced by the charge that he had showed political cowardice, he said, 'I think I can be accused of many things in life but I do not think 'frit' is one of them. I am a fighter and a warrior but I am determined to pick my battles.' It was announced that the original *Star Wars* cast would reunite in 'Star Wars: Episode VII'.

Scott Clissold
Sunday Express
1 May 2014

The public will not be told what George Bush said to Tony Blair in the run up to the Iraq War, despite a request by the official inquiry into the conflict for documents detailing their exchanges to be published. Sir John Chilcot, who heads the inquiry, conceded partial defeat in his attempt to publish records from more than 130 conversations between the former prime minister and then US president.

Bob Moran
The Daily Telegraph
2 May 2014

According to the cartoonist: There was some concern about the fact that many *Telegraph* readers are also UKIP supporters and they might not appreciate the caricatures. But the point of the cartoon, of course, was that, even amongst this lot, Ed Miliband stands out as the 'loon'. I only got a few angry emails.

Peter Schrank
The Independent on Sunday
4 May 2014

Gerry Adams was arrested in connection with one of the most notorious IRA murders of 'the Troubles'. Adams denied any involvement in the killing, but former IRA members have claimed he directed the murder. According to the cartoonist: *The Independent*'s lawyer had to be consulted on this one. I wanted to draw the younger version of Adams with a gun in his hand, but she considered this libellous. She was also worried about the beret, which is traditionally associated with membership of the IRA, but I managed to find a very old photograph of Adams wearing a beret at an IRA funeral. In 1995, at a difficult moment in the Northern Ireland peace process, Adams warned British ministers that 'the IRA haven't gone away, you know'.

Martin Rowson
The Guardian
5 May 2014

Ed Miliband said there needed to be an independent assessment of whether a takeover of the British drug company AstraZeneca by its US rival Pfizer was in the country's national interest: 'No other country in the world would be waving this bid through, nodding it through, on the basis of pretty weak assurances from Pfizer, who have a pretty dubious record when it comes to their record in this country and other takeovers.' No 10 denied Labour claims it is acting as a 'cheerleader' for the deal, saying it is fighting for British jobs and British science.

Dave Brown
The Independent
7 May 2014

According to the cartoonist: As it attempts to reduce the unemployment figures it emerges that the Department for Work and Pensions now intends to sanction claimants if they refuse to take up zero-hours contracts. Also in the news was Prince Harry, the latest in a string of public figures attempting to 'twerk'.

Peter Schrank
The Independent on Sunday
18 May 2014

According to the cartoonist: On the previous weekend I had driven to the north Norfolk coast, then inland from there. It struck me that the further I got into rural areas, the more UKIP posters and hoardings proliferated. Surely in these places immigration can't be a problem, on the contrary, agriculture benefits from cheap eastern European labour. On the other hand Norwich, which I had visited on the way, was dominated by Labour and Green Party posters. It seems that the fear, rather than the reality, of immigration motivates UKIP support.

Bob Moran
The Daily Telegraph
18 May 2014

According to the cartoonist: Another idea that was slightly open to interpretation. The intended message was that the dinosaur continues to survive despite the labels and accusations raining down. Some readers took it to mean that the old fossil was about to be obliterated. Ambiguity's not necessarily a bad thing.

Chris Riddell
The Observer
18 May 2014

An internal Liberal Democrat document revealed that the party was braced for a complete wipeout in the European parliamentary elections. A wipeout, or even a dramatic reduction, in the Lib Dem contingent in the European parliament would represent a serious blow to Nick Clegg's authority. The document also indicated that the Lib Dem leader would forfeit his own Sheffield Hallam constituency at the next election. To make matters worse, Michael Gove's special advisor had been briefing against Clegg over his 'free school meals to infants' policy.

COST OF LIVING EXPERT CAUGHT OUT OVER GROCERY BILL...

THIS CHEESE IS JUST LIKE MY CREDIBILITY, GROMIT...

...WITH ACKNOWLEDGEMENTS...

21 V 14

PeterBrookes

Peter Brookes
The Times
21 May 2014

Ed Miliband told ITV's presenters on *Good Morning Britain* that his family spent £70 to £80 a week on groceries, before being slapped down by presenter Susannah Reid, who told the squirming Labour leader: 'The average weekly bill for a family of four is more than £100. So you're going to be spending significantly more than £70 or £80. People would say one of the problems with politicians is they are actually talking about something but out of touch with the reality, and the reality is that it's much higher than you have quoted.'

Paul Thomas
Daily Express
23 May 2014

Prince Charles's comparison of Vladimir Putin to Adolf Hitler over Russia's annexation of Crimea from Ukraine as 'unacceptable, outrageous and low'. The comments were made by Charles during a conversation with a former Polish war refugee during a royal tour to Canada.

Martin Rowson
The Guardian
24 May 2014

Nigel Farage said UKIP was on track to win the Euro elections, which 'will be an earthquake because never before in the history of British politics has a party seen to be an insurgent party ever topped the polls in a national election'. If the result is confirmed as a UKIP win, it would be the first time since 1984 that the Westminster opposition party, in this instance Labour, has failed to top the poll in the European elections.

Dave Brown
The Independent
30 May 2014

According to the cartoonist: A plot to replace Nick Clegg with Vince Cable runs out of road. Clegg's allies have accused supporters of Vince Cable of plotting to undermine his position as Lib Dem leader. Supporters of Clegg claim Cable is responsible for commissioning opinion polls that suggest the Lib Dems would do better at the general election if they got rid of the present leader.

Bob Moran
The Daily Telegraph
31 May 2014

According to the cartoonist: The image of Farage smugly brandishing his pint of beer after victory in the European elections had been everywhere for a couple of days and this was just a straightforward 'Beer as a metaphor for political success' cartoon. In hindsight, I think the order should be a bit different.

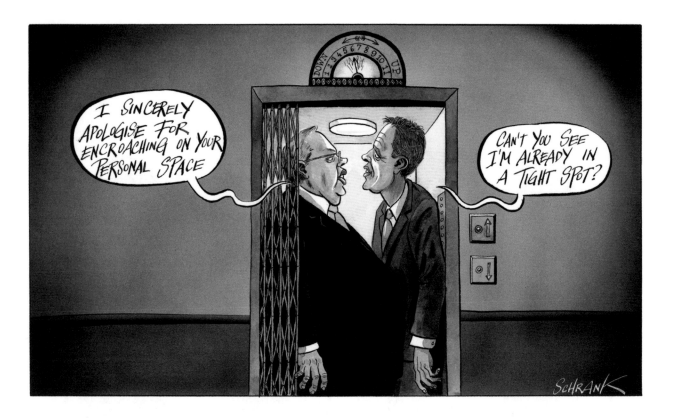

Peter Schrank
*The Independent
on Sunday*
1 June 2014

Lord Rennard still denied sexual harassment, but said he was sorry if he inadvertently encroached on the four women's personal space. After a difficult week for the deputy prime minister, he was now facing a dilemma over whether to reninstate Rennard. Clegg had previously said it would be enough for the party's former chief executive to apologise to the women involved, but they are all calling for him to be permanently excluded from the party.

Morten Morland
The Times
2 June 2014

FIFA's decision to award Qatar with the 2022 World Cup continued to provoke controversy, as a former member of FIFA's executive committee faced fresh allegations of corruption. FIFA president Sepp Blatter said people are trying to destroy football's global governing body, ludicrously claiming attacks on World Cup 2022 host Qatar are motivated by racism and discrimination.

King Juan Carlos I of Spain announced his abdication after 39 years on the throne, to 'open a new era of hope for a younger generation'. The 76-year-old will hand the throne to his son, Prince Felipe, 46, and his glamorous wife Letizia, a former award-winning newsreader and divorcée. He is the third European monarch to abdicate in just over a year, after King Albert II of Belgium gave his crown to son Philippe last July, three months after Queen Beatrix of the Netherlands made way for her firstborn, Prince Willem-Alexander. Juan Carlos, who oversaw his country's transition from dictatorship to democracy, has seen the twilight of his monarchy blighted by scandal and health problems.

Paul Thomas
Daily Express
3 June 2014

146

Dave Brown

The Independent
4 June 2014

According to the cartoonist: Syria, or at least those areas still under government control, goes to the polls to re-elect Bashar al-Assad in a stage-managed show of democracy amid the bloody civil war.

Steve Bell
The Guardian
5 June 2014

Shoppers will be charged 5p for plastic bags as part of a host of new measures announced in the Queen's speech, and the state opening of parliament — the start of the final session of this parliament before the general election.

Steve Bright 'Brighty'
The Sun
8 June 2014

A World War II veteran, who disappeared from his nursing home to attend the D-Day commemorations in France, returned to the UK. Bernard Jordan, 89, left The Pines care home in Hove unannounced on Thursday, and was reported missing to Sussex Police that evening. Staff later discovered he had joined other veterans in France. Chief executive of Gracewell Care Homes, Peter Curtis, said Mr Jordan was 'a bit embarrassed about the fuss' on his return to the UK.

Steve Bell
The Guardian
12 June 2014

The mayor of London Boris Johnson has decided to go ahead and buy water cannons. Johnson had discussed the issue with David Cameron, and the prime minister had backed 'in principle' the mayor acquiring the cannons.

Christian Adams
The Daily Telegraph
13 June 2014

The insurgents, largely Sunni Muslims, advanced into the ethnically diverse province of Diyala, capturing the town of Dhuluiyah, just 60 miles from Baghdad. A spokesman for the militants, who call themselves the Islamic State of Iraq and Syria (ISIS), vowed the group would press on to the capital. Officials said three plane-loads of Americans were evacuated from a major Iraqi air base in Sunni territory to the north of Baghdad.

WARMING UP

BOB 15·06·14

Bob Moran
The Daily Telegraph
15 June 2014

Iran considered the possibility of co-operating with the United States to restore security to Iraq. Asked if Tehran would work with its old adversary the United States in tackling advances by jihadists in Iraq, Iranian President Hassan Rouhani replied: 'We can think about it if we see America starting to confront the terrorist groups in Iraq or elsewhere.'

THE BLAIR PROPERTY PORTFOLIO...

GRADE II LISTED TOWNHOUSE...

MEWS EXTENSION...

IRAQ: I WAS RIGHT

Peter Brookes
The Times
17 June 2014

Tony Blair rejected claims that the 2003 Iraq invasion was to blame for the current crisis gripping the country, pointing the finger instead firmly at the Maliki government and the war in Syria. The latest accounts for Blair's business interests around the world are booming. The accounts, for the 12 months to April 2013, give the best indication yet of Blair's earning power. His wealth, including a London townhouse, a country estate, and several other properties, is estimated at £70 million.

153

Morten Morland
The Times
19 June 2014

Home Secretary Theresa May has apologised for delays in processing passport applications and insisted the government was doing all it could to deal with the situation. Foreign Secretary William Hague revealed that as many as 400 British nationals may be fighting for terrorist groups in Syria. Hague also confirmed that the UK could cancel the passports of any British militants fighting for the terrorist groups in Syria, or the ISIL in Iraq, and would even arrest them.

WISE ED GOES FOR THE YOUTH VOTE

Steve Bell
The Guardian
20 June 2014

Ed Miliband apologised for any offence caused on Merseyside after being photographed with a special World Cup edition of *The Sun*. It has been widely boycotted in Liverpool after it reported lies about Liverpool fans in the wake of the Hillsborough disaster. After a prankster managed to hack into the Labour press team's Twitter account, it seemed that Miliband had come up with his most revolutionary policy so far. 'Everybody should have his own owl,' said the tweet that quickly took flight on social media. The Labour account was quickly deluged by puns.

CAUGHT BETWEEN IRAQ AND A HARD PLACE...

SECTARIANISM

ISIS

BAGHDAD

DAVID SIMONDS

Dave Simonds
The Observer
22 June 2014

ISIS expanded their offensive, capturing three strategic towns, and the first border crossing with Syria to fall on the Iraqi side. It is the latest blow against Prime Minister Nouri al-Maliki, who is fighting for his political life even as forces beyond his control are pushing the country toward a sectarian showdown. According to the cartoonist: Nouri Al Maliki's sectarian policies backfire on both himself and the people of Iraq.

PROPOSED NORTHERN RAIL ROUTE

vote Adams

Christian Adams
The Daily Telegraph
24 June 2014

George Osborne has said the government will consider building a high speed rail link in the North of England, at a cost of around £7 billion. In a speech in Manchester, Osborne said a modern, fast transport network would effectively join several cities into an economic northern powerhouse.

IN A TIGHT SPOT...

Juncker

27 VI 14
Peter Brookes

Peter Brookes
The Times
27 June 2014

Angela Merkel made it clear that David Cameron would fail if he tried to stop the nomination of Jean-Claude Juncker as the next head of the European Commission. Cameron had vowed to block his candidacy as he viewed him as too much of an old-style federalist who would obstruct his push to reform the EU.

BLUELOU

Lou McKeever 'Bluelou'
Morning Star
28 June 2014

Former *News of the World* editor Rebekah Brooks was cleared after an eight-month trial on charges of conspiring to hack phones, bribe officials, and obstruct police. The hacking scandal had sent tremors through the top of British politics. Brooks is a friend and neighbour of David Cameron, and Andy Coulson was Cameron's director of communications for a number of years.

Martin Rowson
The Guardian
30 June 2014

Former education secretary David Blunkett said Prince Charles tried to influence policy, while others said he lobbied on GM and alternative medicine. Recalling his conversations with Prince Charles, Blunkett said, 'I would explain that our policy was not to expand grammar schools, and he didn't like that.' Jon Cruddas accused Miliband's inner circle of wielding a 'profound dead hand at the centre' to stop the party adopting bold policies.

Peter Brookes
The Times
1 July 2014

Alex Salmond hailed the 700th anniversary of the Battle of Bannockburn, reminding people of its importance to Scotland. Jihadist militant group ISIS said that it had establishd a caliphate, or Islamic state, on the territories it controls in Iraq and Syria. It also proclaimed the group's leader, Abu Bakr al-Baghdadi, as caliph and 'leader for Muslims everywhere'.

L'ÉLECTION
2017

LES
ALLÉGATIONS

ADAMS

Christian Adams
The Daily Telegraph
2 July 2014

Ex-French president Nicolas Sarkozy was placed under formal investigation over alleged influence peddling. He appeared before a judge in Paris after 15 hours of questioning by anti-corruption police. This is thought to have been the first time a former French head of state has been held in police custody.

Christian Adams
The Daily Telegraph
3 July 2014

Andy Murray's defence of his Wimbledon title was ended by Grigor Dimitrov in the quarter-final. It followed closely on from England's football team's exit from the World Cup in Brazil in the group stage, failing to win a match, and losing to Italy and Uruguay. In the same month, England's cricket team lost the test series against Sri Lanka, while the rugby union players lost their test series in New Zealand, 3-0. The Tour de France was about to begin in Leeds.

Steve Bell
The Guardian
4 July 2014

George Osborne failed to answer a question from a seven-year-old schoolboy while being interviewed on live TV. Sam Raddings politely asked the chancellor, who has a degree in modern history from Oxford, what seven times eight is. 'I've made it a rule in life not to answer a whole load of maths questions,' Osborne replied.

Ben Jennings
i newspaper
6 July 2014

According to the cartoonist: This was one of those cartoon ideas that came to me at the last minute just before I sent a few mediocre rough ideas to my editor on what had been a slow news day. When news came in that Andy Coulson had been sent to prison, I was trying to think of a way of showing Coulson up to his old phone-hacking antics whilst in the slammer. I thought that when Coulson is asked to hand over his personal possessions before being led to prison, he could hand over his phone as well as the officer's, but then I came up with the better idea of him eavesdropping the cliché of prisoners and their phone calls.

7/7 GARYBARKER

Gary Barker
The Times
7 July 2014

According to the cartoonist: In the wake of allegations of historical child abuse, the shadow of justice begins to fall over Parliament. Many people feel politicians think they don't have to abide by the same rules the rest of us do and hope the investigations will finally show that they have to live by the same laws as the rest of us.

An eye for a tooth ... a hand for an eye ...
.. a life for a hand ... a people for a life ...

Dave Brown
The Independent
9 July 2014

As Hamas rockets targeted Israel's major cities, Israel continued its intensive air bombardment of Gaza. Benjamin Netanyahu vowed to increase the assault on Hamas and the terrorist organisations in Gaza. This cartoon was criticised in the Israeli press for being an 'outrageous and morally contorted cartoon'. According to Eylon Aslan-Levy, a member of the Board of Deputies of British Jews, in order to characterise Israel's actions, Brown has misused the 'eye for an eye' verse from Jewish scripture: 'mistakenly taken it as an injunction for pointless retribution rather than proportional punishment'.

Martin Rowson
The Guardian
11 July 2014

Israel's bombardment of Gaza in a bid to end Hamas rocket attacks was about to enter its fifth day. Wimbledon officials denied that the spate of high-profile withdrawals from this year's championship was a direct reaction to the controversial new seeding system.

Peter Schrank
The Independent on Sunday
13 July 2014

David Cameron and Nick Clegg announced plans for emergency spy laws at a press conference in Number 10. Cameron insisted that new laws were needed to reinstate powers to 'help keep us safe from those who would harm UK citizens'. The laws will be rushed through Parliament amid mounting concern about the threat posed to the UK by jihadists returning from fighting in Syria.

CHIEF WHIP

ELECTION 2015

Christian Adams
The Daily Telegraph
16 July 2014

Michael Gove was demoted from his dream post as a radical education secretary to a lower role of chief whip, as David Cameron attempted to neutralise the Tories' increasingly toxic relations with the teaching profession. Cameron had also grown increasingly frustrated with Gove in recent months after he had confronted fellow cabinet ministers in public.

Dave Brown
The Independent
18 July 2014

The Labour Party accused the Lib Dems of 'unbelievable hypocrisy' over its change in stance on the bedroom tax. Nick Clegg said that the Lib Dems no longer supported the policy in its current form and now wanted an exemption for disabled people, and for housing benefit to only be cut if households refuse an offer to move. The proposals are expected to be part of the party's 2015 election manifesto.

Peter Brookes
The Times
19 July 2014

Barack Obama accused Russia of supplying arms to the separatist rebels who had shot down Malaysian Airways flight MH17 out of the sky over Ukraine, killing 298 passengers on board. Downing Street claimed that it appeared 'increasingly likely that MH-17 was shot down by a separatist missile' fired from near Torez, an area controlled by pro-Russian rebels.

172

Peter Schrank
The Independent on Sunday
20 July 2014

Global leaders put pressure on Vladimir Putin, as armed separatists continued to block international inspectors attempting to identify and repatriate bodies at the Malaysia Airlines crash site. Amid reports that pro-Russia rebels had removed corpses themselves and were looting credit cards and other possessions belonging to some of the 298 victims, the Dutch prime minister said that Putin had 'one last chance to show he means to help'. According to the cartoonist: Unfortunately it's often the depressing events that bring out the best in me.

THE 'SELFIE'...

Me + my bezzie Mate Obama!

Dave Brown
The Independent
22 July 2014

Ed Miliband met Barack Obama at the White House for just 25 minutes in what is known as a 'brush-by'. Asked if having his photograph taken with the US President was simply a photo opportunity, Miliband said: 'As somebody who wants to be the prime minister in less than 10 months' time, it's important I'm here talking to key figures in the administration about the many pressing issues that our country faces and indeed the world faces.'

Boris Johnson indicated he might pull out of a tennis match that was bought for £160,000 by the wife of a former minister in Vladimir Putin's government. Lubov Chernukhin had bid at a Tory fundraising auction for a tennis match with David Cameron and Boris Johnson. Cameron rejected calls to pay back the donation. He said he would not accept money from a 'Putin crony', but Mrs Chernukhin's husband, Vladimir, 'certainly wasn't that'.

Steve Bell
The Guardian
24 July 2014

Peter Brookes
The Times
25 July 2014

The al-Wafa hospital grounds in Gaza City, and its immediate surroundings, were being repeatedly used by Hamas and the Palestinian Islamic jihadists as a command center, rocket launching site, and a post enabling terrorists to open fire at Israeli forces.

The International Monetary Fund disclosed that Britain's economy grew faster than those of every other major developed country and as a consequence upgraded its forecast for UK growth to 3.2 per cent this year. A Policy agenda to tackle low pay, by Lancaster University, revealed that despite the economic recovery, the UK still lacked an effective strategy for dealing with the challenge of low paid work. The report's authors highlighted that low pay now affects 5.1 million employees (21%) of the workforce, and that over a quarter of low-paid workers remained stuck in low pay for over a decade.

Chris Riddell
The Observer
27 July 2014

Martin Rowson
The Guardian
28 July 2014

During a BBC television interview, Andrew Marr presented Ed Miliband with cartoons of him as 'Wallace' by Peter Brookes. Marr then asked his guest if he felt 'hurt' by his portrayal in the media, as they discussed Miliband's image problem, adding, 'You have very poor leadership ratings at the moment.' Attempting to shrug off his embarrassment, the Labour leader said, 'I didn't realise you were going to bring me a present; that's kind. I'll show it to my kids.'

Brian Adcock
The Independent
28 July 2014

Nick Clegg called for Russia to be removed as hosts of the 2018 World Cup after the shooting down of a Malaysia Airlines flight over eastern Ukraine. Football's world governing body FIFA ruled out calls for Russia to be boycotted, insisting the tournament could be 'a force for good'. Clegg said that allowing it to go ahead without a change of course by President Vladimir Putin would make the world look 'so weak and so insincere' in its condemnation of Moscow's annexation of Crimea and support for the rebels.

Secretary-General Ban Ki-moon reinforced the Security Council's call for an immediate and unconditional humanitarian cease-fire in the Gaza war, demanding that Israel and Hamas end the violence 'in the name of humanity.' The UN chief accused Israeli Prime Minister Benjamin Netanyahu and Hamas leader Khaled Mashaal of being irresponsible and 'morally wrong' for letting their people get killed in the conflict. He urged them to demonstrate 'political will' and 'compassionate leadership' to end the suffering of war-weary citizens.

Peter Brookes
The Times
29 July 2014

'Oh dear. That'll cost you. Visiting time ended three minutes ago.'

Stan McMurtry 'Mac'
Daily Mail
1 August 2014

According to the *Daily Mail*, wardens at Southport and Ormskirk Hospitals are encouraged to issue tickets to vulnerable people and take pictures at dodgy angles to make offences seem worse than they actually are.

GAS

Dave Brown
The Independent
2 August 2014

As the anniversary of the outbreak of World War I grew nearer, world leaders seemed incapable of dealing with the ongoing crises in Gaza, Iraq, Syria, and the Ukraine.

Chris Riddell
The Observer
3 August 2014

Israeli defence forces in Gaza found a Hamas manual on 'urban warfare', which explained how the civilian population can be used against IDF forces and revealed that Hamas knew the IDF is committed to minimising harm to civilians. Hamas had been continuously using Palestinian civilians in Gaza as human shields. Israel had widely derided Hamas for what it called a 'human shields' policy, hiding its military assets and firing from behind civilian sites including mosques, schools, and hospitals.

THE PALESTINIAN DEFENCE DOME

GARYBARKER

Gary Barker
The Times
4 August 2014

According to the cartoonist: While the argument raged about proportionate response, the death count among innocent Palestinians killed by Israeli missiles, not protected by an 'Iron Dome' defence system, continued to massively and disproportionately mount.

Ed Miliband said David Cameron's 'silence' on Israel's ongoing offensive in Gaza was 'inexplicable', insisting the prime minister must publicly oppose the deaths of 'hundreds of innocent Palestinians'. This cartoon was published on the 100th anniversary of the outbreak of World War I. According to the cartoonist: To fuse the two stories of the day: the WWI centenary and a Downing Street row over Cameron's silence regarding Israel's bombardment of Gaza, I decided to pastiche an iconic WWI propaganda poster for the visual. It's always fun as a cartoonist when you get the chance to modernise an old, recognisable work of art and this is an image that has always fascinated me.

Ben Jennings
The Guardian
4 August 2014

Peter Brookes
The Times
6 August 2014

Baroness Warsi resigned from the government, saying its policy on the crisis in Gaza was 'morally indefensible'.
David Cameron 'regretted' that she had not discussed her decision to quit with him before announcing it.
Several backbench Conservative MPs had called on Cameron to take a more robust line with Israel amid
concerns its actions in Gaza were 'disproportionate'.

Christian Adams
The Daily Telegraph
7 August 2014

Boris Johnson ended months of speculation by saying he would seek to become an MP again at next year's general election. But he said it was 'highly unlikely' he would one day stand to become Conservative leader, replacing David Cameron, as there was 'no vacancy'. Cameron, who was on holiday in Portugal, instantly tweeted: 'Great news that Boris plans to stand at next year's general election - I've always said I want my star players on the pitch.'

Brian Adcock
The Independent
8 August 2014

More than 200 British celebrities, including Mick Jagger, signed a letter urging Scotland to stick with the United Kingdom in September's independence referendum. The open letter was signed by Oscar, Grammy, and Nobel Prize winners, Olympic gold medallists, lords, knights of the realm, professors, and novelists — representing 'the best of British talent and intellect', according to the organisers.

Morten Morland
The Times
9 August 2014

After months of hesitation, President Obama authorised the use of airstrikes against Islamic militants in Iraq who had overrun large parts of the country, threatening tens of thousands of Iraqi civilians trapped atop a barren mountain, where they sought refuge after fleeing their homes. Islamic State fighters, who have beheaded and crucified captives in their drive to eradicate unbelievers, have advanced to within a half hour's drive of Arbil, the capital of Iraq's Kurdish region and a hub for United States oil companies.

Peter Schrank
The Independent on Sunday
10 August 2014

Alex Salmond continued to refuse to name his 'Plan B' currency for a separate Scotland after his surprise defeat to Alistair Darling in the independence TV debate. According to the cartoonist: A really important story, two radically different and very caricaturable politicians, fantastic landscape and a nice, smutty (if slightly overused) joke: some cartoons are just great fun to draw.

STORMY TIMES.....

Brian Adcock
The Independent
11 August 2014

Having just resigned as a Cabinet minister over the UK's policy on Gaza, Baroness Warsi broadened her criticisms of her party by saying it would not win the next election unless it did more to attract ethnic minority voters. She told *The Sunday Times* and *The Independent on Sunday* the Tories had left it 'a little late' to woo ethnic minorities for the next election. In her newspaper interviews she also criticised 'bitchy' male colleagues and repeated her anger at the government's handling of the fighting in Gaza.

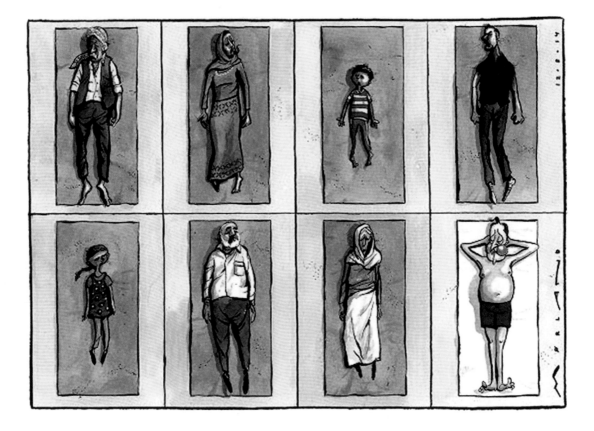

A number of Tory backbench MPs criticised David Cameron for allowing himself to be photographed on a Portuguese beach while RAF crews were flying dangerous missions to drop humanitarian supplies to refugees trapped in Iraq. In order to shame the prime minister into cutting his holiday short, these MPs distributed this cartoon to other members of the Conservative Party. As a direct result, David Cameron returned to Downing Street from his holiday a day earlier than expected so as to assume direct command of the government's response to the Iraq crisis.

Morten Morland
The Times
12 August 2014

CARTOONISTS